UPS AND DOWNS

ups and downs

jake kooistra

Contents

I	anxitey	1
II	depression	5
III	other side of anxitey & depression	9
IV	how i ended up here	13
V	anger and hurt	22
VI	god and forgiving	29
VII	friends that never leave	32
VIII	only the start	36
IX	unloving	39
X	hard love	43
XI	friends side of my life	46
XII	the person that helps	48
XIII	new start	50

I

anxitey

as i said in the first book what ive seen been threw the pain this is for you to get how it feels to have the fear and sadness it comes with for my 4 years ive had sadness feeling lonely and the anxitey i never thought all this can hurt people and how bad it can really get till ive lived it and hurt people i always had some kinda stress from work life getting into things i should not of we all think it can stop us but it stopped me in my tracks i never would think it could stop me in my tracks like it did i was always thinking it cant hurt me but the week it got worse i was at fires having fun till fights would happen and guns and i never thought it would happen my stress started then bad got away from it was fine went to wawa for some food and someone tried to hit a good friend of mine for closing his truck door so the guy could get out i sat there knowing something was gonna happen and it did he pulled a gun to my friends face i rushed to my truck to get mine to stop him someone called the cops and they showed up right before he was gonna hurt him i put mine away and cop said are you the one we all said no we had ours incase they tackled the kid comes to find out he had 2 of them and fake id to save him self and we all were over stressed i sat there thinking this might be it if he turns at me before they got there i was scared from that day on ant small thing would scare me some one would walk up and i dont know i would get scared if someone gave me a dirty look i was thinking of that hole night so like ive said before before i got like this we went to a fire for a birthday and my anxitey hit wrong cause we were stuck the fear of it happening again was ptsd for me ever since i had that happen ive had major anxitey scared to leave in fear of it happening again i think the fear never really goes away i think it will always be around i think we always have this in our mind that anxitey is just us doing it to our self but its really not we have this in our minds and people tell us we are crazy we can get rid of it truly we cant anxitey is like a see threw wall we dont try to think about it but when we hit the wall it comes falling down no matter how hard we try to not let it i feel like everything may end up hurting me and ill never be able to get passed it once it happen people like to think anxitey is a joke or not real but really its not its not us we dont wanna live with it our brains sooner or later takes it over and everything becomes a fear to us mine has been driving i used to love to drive anywhere any time any place i was always wanting to drive far and not care and after all this driving has been really hard i cant make it but to a spot i can make it 10 min down the road but only at night no street lights cause at night when its late no ones out its just me and the road and the lights in my small town here or there will be a car but not alot i always looked before i felt for turn arounds so if i got bad i could turn around and go home when im leaving and going away from home i get scared hearts racing but i push threw once im out for a few im fine but when im on my way home it stops its like my body knows im going home where its safe when people i know try to come over my body freaks its like im scared on what they think after this happen or what will they say i always try to over come it when they are here im fine or they have to show up without me knowing so i cant say no or freak out about it i think its a new way i have to learn so i dont let it run my life anxitey is no joke its not fun makes you think your crazy and makes you wonder will it ever stop but you have to learn to control it and i still am to this day and im sure i will for a long time

II

depression

    depression for me is like a jail even tho ive never been but its 4 walls that are the same you feel trapped behind these bars you try so hard to escape and just like jail its hard to escape my sadness came from pain i did to people to my family thinking i was better then everyone i knew my heart was kind and pure but with all this im numb im lost im not me and all i want is me back i lost some i dearly loved to the damn thing called covid and thats when i lost myself the happy me the kind heart i had i would say things push people away leave them like its nothing i never would of Guessed in a my life that much pain can do that to a person mine is like a black hole ive made it out 3 times once alone twice with help and this time is not the same i dont want help i just want to be left but i dont i pray alot for god to help me out of this hole the pain im in hurts the mind controls me and how i feel and how i wanna love how i wanna treat people some days for me are better then most me and my mom get along but sometimes my sadness turn to anger and hurts her she hates seeing her baby boy like this like every mom would i think if i was in her place i would fall apart not knowing if im not helping if i push to hard but for my mom she never does i just let the pain control me and i hate it i stop it but it hurts worse i learn every day how to control it with less pain each time the pain love is kind love is patient it does not envy but love can fail like this when you cant see it when you cant feel it when your heart goes cold when you feel like can anyone really love me? is there enough love for me to give to anyone or am i just a lost hope will there ever be hope for the love i once had for people or will i never want it again ? love everyone you can i think the thing i learned the most was knowing one day we wont have best friend our mom dad sister brother love them while you can dont let this mind battle win you over so you end up losing the ones you love and never get to live and not let this take your life over its never over pray to god like i did ask for help dont be scared to ask him for help and that goes for friends and family always live and love it will also help you threw all this its never over there is more life to live love is kind and will wait and one day is a day when depression hits your days blend together you see life is passing by faster then we think we all wont be around forever but we need to realize to slow down and spend time with people one day they can be here next there gone i never looked at life that way till i lost my nana she was my life and i wish i would of stayed around her more i came home went to bed or was out half the time after work and i wish i would of slowed down little did i know it was gonna be her last halloween my last birthday with her christmas

III

other side of anxitey & depression

life was going right, everything was moving in a motion that seemed just right. but all because of something happening it changed everything. anxiety and depression is a serious thing that someone can go through. and it hurts when it's the person that you love most. but it hurts even worse when this person doesn't realize how bad they are hurting you when they are hurting themselves by going what they go through. anxiety and depression wins. it wins your mental health, your physical health, you happiness, your ability to want to do things, and your relationships.

i've learned this the past 11 months. it's hard being the person in the relationship with the person who goes through all of this on a daily basis. you take a beating, not physically but mentally. even when you try your best to be there for that person. depression especially ruins more than you can imagine. it will ruin your ability to feel for someone, be there for someone, and especially the ability for that person to love someone. i was loved by this person like no other person has loved me before, but then depression won. it took it all, and that's something that is very hard to get past. and it's not this one persons fault that this is happening, they try to fight it but it doesn't work. and it takes a hell of a person to be able to sit by the side of someone who goes through this. even if they tell you they don't love you anymore. but you still dig down knowing it's the depression talking not them.

you'll truly never know what's actually going on. one day, your just there. the next they are asking you to marry them. then your back to just being there. feeling pushed aside, because they are scared to lean on you. even tho you promise to be there. no matter what. loving someone is a hard thing to do, especially when you are raising their baby, while trying to make sure they are still your priority, so they don't feel like your letting them down. a lot of arguments come with this, but you have to find a way to make it through and know neither of you are meaning what you are saying. this person's depression is talking in the argument, and you just don't know how to say the right things because you don't know what goes on in there head and what makes them upset. it's all a guessing game. your heart stays broken for a while, because your so lost on what's going on but you know it's not them so you hold on until you and this person are back to the way you should be, when they can finally put it behind them and not let the depression over come them. yes it'll always be there, but not as bad. but you'll wait as long as you can for this person because they are truly the one person you love more than anything. it's hard truly loving a person with depression. but no matter what, you won't let go. you'll love this person just as much, if not more.

IV

how i ended up here

Life can be good but sometimes it goes bad My head is like a clock that's stopped I always feel like crap my nausea won't go away my Anxitey my fear of things that never used to scare me have taken over my life little things cause it all people coming to see me me leaving the house I wanna hide away not eat from the nausea where on the other hand i wanna eat all foods in site I never wanna leave my bed The bed is my safe place but I get tired of looking at the same old apps the same old videos the consent wanting to do something but the nausea takes my fear to another level & the Anxitey when trying to leave controls it all I feel at peace at night only until my body says your clock stopped again my fear of all this has taken my life away

The back story
was I was a 19-20 year old man having my life
go right for half of my 19 years of age
till January of 23 I was healthy I would eat anything
drink sodas sometimes even beer but not a lot I
always went to bonfires and never was home I
worked at boston whaler for awhile then I went
to p&s hated it always had lack of energy never
thought anything of it that's why boston whaler
was night shift I've been a night person hate
morning I stayed up till 2-4 am half the time
always was at a place called Wawa every day
before work or after work and when I didn't
work it's where I hung out with a-lot of people I
no longer talk to and I hold a-lot of memories
with them there was some I will forever hold
onto

I was the wild one I've been battling depression for a while but never really bothered me cause I was always out doing stuff so it never came across my mind till I was alone but I never really was alone 90% of the time I never let anyone go alone & 2022 I met a lot of good people some became like brothers some became like sister and some used me I was always there for them even the ones I knew would not do the same one night I was home with my gf and it was late I got a call saying my friends bf and his friend flipped there car and we didn't know where they were I called my close friends Zack and Jess and said I need help finding them we only know where they could been

but we drove
for a bit fast in the middle of the highway they
didn't wanna go get checked out till we left I got
a call cause we were headed to wawa to see how
they were doing but got a call they wanted to go
now so we went I didn't feel great as it was head
was full but I went awayways her bf went in but
the driver didn't I won't say names but he didn't
go in he was bleeding everywhere touching me
and part of me thinks he could of gave me HEP
B from his blood doctors think I'm crazy for
thinking that but that was early thanksgiving
morning this all happen but we ended up going
home I was ok I was dealing with some stuff
started working at Walmart built my truck we
went to see christmas lights with friends and
everyone found out I was having a boy in this
timeline life was good I was happy

till I started feeling bad and left my job right before I got sick 20 days go by we ended up going to a fire for a friends birthday and at this point I was having random spells of nausea and never could figure it out when I wanted to get checked out I never did something was stopping me I got scared and I was not sure why Now we go to the fire and I had nausea after dinner and felt bad but it stopped and we went to it mind you it was not far from my house but the dirt road was 1 1/2 lanes could not fit 2 trucks there was some people there that I didn't get along with so we kinda waiting back till my friends showed up to go say hi but my gf at this time had to pee bad so I was stressing cause she was pregnant and she was stressing so it made it worse on me we stayed for a hour saw some people

we were
leaving but people were blocking everything so I
started getting something I never did Anxitey
bad we had to yell at people and I was scared
for the first time in my life I didn't know that
night was gonna be my last night like that we
went home I started feeling like crap smoked my
cigarette showered then ended up passing out
being so tired little did I know what I was gonna
wake up to was gonna be hell I woke up that
morning to all this stuff nausea fast heart rates
didn't wanna eat felt bad didn't wanna drink get
out of bed let alone do anything I was weak 1
week goes by I'm getting out of bed somewhat
just to go to bathroom like we all have to
can't not do that even tho I didn't so I would go
sit outside with mom for a bit to get some air 3
weeks go by and

it's February 9th we called the
3 numbers to come get me I was just the same
but I was at least getting out of bed at this point
so they asked me all the normal stuff what's
going on when this happen they called me crazy
for waiting as long as I did but they loaded me
up and we left mind you I could not drive or
have someone take me and got my blood taken
and other stuff got told it was just Anxitey but
that was not the case but I took the meds they
gave me for it it made me loopy and we went
home woke up feeling good from the meds and
the saline flush they did I felt great again till a
week or so it went back down went to doctor
said it was Anxitey still wanted more on why the
nausea was not stopping next one said a stomach problem but never
looked just went off how
I felt gave me meds didn't take them cause they
were not 100%

Now all this the time till nov I'm having nausea still and to learn to drive at night still can't go far and go out much but I try to keep pushing but along the way of all this I started finding god and Learning more cause my nana before she passed was always into him and trying to teach me but like every teen I didn't want to and I wish I did but now I found him in this hard Time and I won't let go now sometimes I forget to talk to him I still do sins and I try to do better but we are not gonna be sin free at least I think before him going threw all this my depression got bad from not being able to go out and get my mind of everything cause I'm not who I used to be I'll get better then bad again it's a hit or miss but this nausea has controlled my life so far and I hate it and never wish it on anyone Someday I'll be normal I pray everyday for it to wake up like this was all a dream it felt like jail like this always in my room could not leave my body was on lock down didn't do much till I started making my self do it and I still over do it a lot and I try to push more so that when I do it again it will be easy the next few times like when I drive but it's been hard my son is 5 months when I wrote this and he helped me threw alot friends come by sometimes to see me late at night cause I wake up at 12:30 and I'm ok kinda from 2-6 pm then I lay down and feel bad again till about 10-11 pm then I'm up till 4 am and some nights I don't feel good still and some days the same thing and I still wonder why all this happen It scares me everyday this could be my life anymore some days I have doubts like everyone does and some days when I feel good I feel like there's light coming in and maybe this is god clearing a better way of life for me from my past and without him I would not be here

V

anger and hurt

The anger built up inside someone with all I've had go on is very scary the Anxitey makes you wanna say things you don't mean the depression makes you think your worthless in this world and you would be better off not here but it's more then that we are all worthy of this life we turn to bad things to cope with the pain and the anger but little do we think in that time we hurt the ones we love and have to support us
Sooner or later we end up losing them from what we do & say to them and we get worse cause we lose people and think like this because it's what we know to do
In this life

we always push our selfs to the breaking point
or someone we met that don't know your story ends up doing
it by saying the wrong words & doing the wrong things to
you but we break at the point we shouldn't sometimes you
have to take a step back from it all we all need space and
we all make mistakes I've had a bad past on hurting people

loved dearly she helped me threw my depression and when we broke up it all came right back down and the 2nd time around we tried I messed up and hurt her and I never forgive myself for the things I've done to people I've done things in life to think this is my karma but I think also god removed me from ones I was always with so the pain didn't keep tearing me inside when I could not see it myself but it's life and it's scary I still have a lot of bad days and good days I always push to be better and I always ending up failing and I think it's like trying to fix something and you don't know what happen to it in the first place I always say life is short but sometimes it gets slowed down to keep it from being so short so nothing hurts you to end have it end early and depression can do it but I think it also builds us there's a lot of people that try to sugar coat it all but I'm here telling you about what I've gone threw to help if your ever stuck in a place where everything seems so dark & hard to escape it so we lean on things we shouldn't drinking smoking cutting but truly I learned to do it without it all and it's made it better cause I don't wake up worse cause all it does is helps you till it slowly fades away and your suddenly worse and I turned to god for help and a-lot of people don't think he hears us or thinks of us but he does we may not think of it or we see the things he does but what we asked for is in front of us and we don't realize it I didn't see I was getting better till I slowed down and seen everything was how I asked I may not be my self with my health 100% but I sure am glad I took time to realize I was getting myself back & thanks to to people that I pushed away and did things to and they still never left me I think sometimes we have to push people away to see who really stays with us threw it all

sometimes they leave and we
get more sad but they really cared would they of left ? Or
would they have stood by your side no matter what you said
did or pushed them ? Only true ones stay for you and a lot of
them want to help but never forget about them if they ever
go threw it just cause your better don't mean you leave them
behind always help others in need of your help now like I
said I've hurt people in my past way you never should and
never got to say sorry for it all and

sometimes it's better like
that but sometimes for you to move on and heal it takes that
little thing to help it all flow down stream and not get stuck
at the single rock in your way and that's where I'm stuck depression is
like jail
4 walls you see everyday same apps you
use same people you talk to same people you see on social
media it's all the same when your like that we never get out
of bed or wanna do much it's like we are trapped in hole and
we need to fix it by taking care of ourselves

VI

god and forgiving

my nana passed away in 2021 she was my life line and never let me fall apart i was never really sad with her around so when i lost her i lost my self now most people say there mom is there other half but she was mine and my mom and i never got along sometimes but when our world came crashing down we leaned on one and other we never left each other we always found a way to stayed close we built our bond back like a mother and son should we always loved one and other and the loss helped us sadly thats what it took for us to and i wish it didnt happen that way i wish i would of said sorry more times not say the things i said to her and the pain i caused her but god helped us get back and forgive each other like we should of sooner i think everyone dont get along with there family at some points but we have to remember its there first time living two we think they have it all down cause there older then us but they really dont non of us do

we think we know more then them cause we are
younger but we dont either they know more when it comes
to things we know more then they do in parts we all go threw
things that someone else has not been threw but if we just sit
down and learn each other we can pass what we know to our
kids and we teach them they help us understand and we pass
it down from your dads dad to hom to us to our kids they
they do the same and from our moms mom to her to us to our
kid again some of us dont have both parents in our life some
have both some lost one or the other we have to think to our
selfs is this worth being sad about angry about do we really
need to do all that and lose the ones we love to be sorry for
what we did or said god has his plans and we need to know
every day we are here is because of that man this world is
filled with hate for everyone in the world people hate god
cause they think he dont see us or why would this happen to
me but its his plan and if you slow down and let him take you
the way your meant to we would be happy if you keep praying loving
each person
and

stop hating and always forgive
not seek revenge to someone but forgive them we all would
be happy but in this day in age we think hating is normal
and its not thats far from it we all think this life sucks but we
seek the things that god says not to partys hating drinking
fighting we are not meant to hurt another person god will
handle it for us we dont need to take risk life over the things
thats normal and im 21 and been threw it all and its not
worth it thats why im here telling my story my side of it all
we never will live our full life if we are always risking it all
on things we dont need to be risking god works in ways we
dont know cause the world has shown us a diffrent side of it
we live in his world the things in it are not from him or what
we wants from us

VII

friends that never leave

this book ive talked alot about god forgiving
love anxitey sadness anger now its time for friends ive had
alot of friends ill never talk to i have friends that are still
around for me threw it all i hold alot of there deep secrets
ones that are still around and some that have moved on and
we no longer talk or some that are around but not like we
used to be ive had some great times with alot of them and
some bad but theres a few i wanna talk about that are still
around ally has been one of my rocks threw everything just
like jess ry hailey and allison ally is one of those friends you
cant keep away she puts her self threw so much for others
and gets hurt but still has a great heart threw it all she
checks up the most shes been around for awhile she never
fail so call if im in need she checks to make sure i dont ned
anything she talks if i need help she always is by my side
shesone of the sweetest girls youll see shes smart outgoing
will tell you the truth

and not hide it to make you feel better
about something she never fails to be there when needed.
jess is the same way shes been around longer we have had
our ups and downs but shes still amazing she and i dont talk
like we used to but when we are together its like nothing
happen. ry shes amazing in her own way shes outgoing also
but can be a pain but never fails to check up she and i get into
it over dumb stuff but we fix it she always ask about people
i know how there doing shes always there when needed.
hailey is a newer one but she always talks to me tells me if
im being dumb or if i need to talk about stuff but shes great
with always being there. allison and i became friends out of
no were she came into my life when i was alone and scared
when all my problems happen she always talks to me till
she got super busy building her life and she helped me more
then i thought i needed she told me to always keep my head
up keep pushing when i started doing more

after all this she
would always tell me how proud she was and so would ally
& jess & hailey & a man name chase that has stuck threw
it all we were brothers fast we always worked on the trucks
and when we had no one left we had each other we always
talk he always shows up out of no were to see me and its not
what we used to be after all thats happen but we slowly are
going back i know all them hate seeing me like this they miss
the old jake that was always crazy funny always wanting to
have fun and hang out they tell me they miss who i was
before this they all pray for me and i know when i come back
ill have the warm welcome and

it will be life again like we knew it some things will change now that i have my son and i wont be out all night but i know they wont care because im back to me we all were close we had a great friend group we all would go bowling sit at wawa go to fair go eat go do late night walks on canal but the best was flagler ave we knew so many people but most of all our beach days and we all did alot no matter whos not friends with who if i called them all together we would be back but turely i have some of the best of friends i could ask for and if one day i lose some of them a part of me will forever hold onto them for everything they have done for me.

VIII

only the start

this past 11 months is only the start to my life it maybe bad right now but it will get better and the start will come when god knows im ready not when i think i am i know this book has not alot of pages but this is only 1 of them i love doing this and it maybe short but i fit alot into this and i hope this helps learn into my life before i get to the next book so everyone knows this i know should help alot of people threw some stuff and thats my goal is to be able to do that for others and know i tried to help as much as i could i hope people learn lifes not simple or to hard but we make it harder if you slow down and relax you can see life is not all that bad it maybe at some times but life treats us just fine for alot there are alot of people that aint so lucky they have to be taken care of all the time people make fun of them but you have to know they are just like me and you we all are made withe the same parts we all have hearts lungs eyes bones blood everything is the same and

we treat them like there not like us like we
are higher then they are theres so many people in this world
and we fouces on the bad things not god but we should i do
and its the best thing ive done if everyone would get along
and treat people like they want to be and trust god we would
all have a better world and without that this woreld will fall
apart we think the world has been the same but its not

IX

unloving

I found love in us when I shouldn't of you were my heart our love was like the sand and the stars we started off with nothing not knowing much we were on and off 3 times every time people got in the way and you were not wanting the love I was giving to you with every noise and every love story ours felt like a movie where we can't stay apart our chapter was short I let go scared of you leaving for collage love I had for you was like non ever our love was scary happy fun thrilling but toxic in the end couldn't stay apart and still if you came back I would let you back in hoping we rewrite our story the right way no wrong ways we both know we will always want the other person some people don't see things we did over love was pure I could not imaged another day without you till I had to

There's a lot of things I could say about us but this book
would not hold the pages of it all I still remembered the
times we fell apart but picked it back up and each time it was
better we were always talking about kids a joke for us how
we would have everything we wanted the spark we had with
only talking on the phone it was a bad year for the world so
everything was shut untill we both snuck out and I met you
at our spot on the water where there was dolphins everytime
we seen the water together like it was our sigh the time
your parents found us there at 7 am and I was knee deep in the
water and we still laugh about it to this day me and you when
we talk there's was no love like your mom gave me and she
always said she loved me the most and I know she still does
to this day I love her and her cooking your little brother was
the best to have around I loved when it was us 3 or me and
him but most of all I loved how we were all like family

From canoe's on the water in the rain getting stuck on shells and me and jas had to step on them to help everyone and at that moment I knew I was gonna marry you i never stood up like that for anyone and we had to protect ry little man and her mom the way I loved everyone and had it all in return was the best I think if collage was never there we would of made it the last time I was scared to let someone I love and still do go that far knowing some man can get you and he did but there will be love forever we always used val and vlad to sneak around. Let's go back to the trip on the canoes in oak hill Florida with the water lighting up every time you touched it and that beautiful smile that lights us the hole world was big as ever from the day I left you the 2nd time was selfish but it made me grow as a person but we always run back and I hate it but I love it

We met a lot of new people we grew together in the truck world we were known as them everyone loved us i met my brother threw you Kris was my brother and me and rylee sent up something special for her dad and I was the the only one to do that on July 4th 2021 I looked at you as you would cry and know I'm still lucky to have you in my life our love was one I never seen before I cared more about you the I did about my self I could talk about the time we went to the arcade the 2nd time we tried us again it was a stressful night cause I had you back I always seem to be on track when you were with me and when you weren't I fell off my tracks and im till stuck to this day no knowing what I need. You the other girl but I always think of you ry this book is to show how love can be crazy the love and "unlove" of someone.

X

hard love

love is a toxic thing i found that out every time ive been inlove it shows me why i hate opening my self we all do when you see the people you loved leave lie to your face there was this girl that said i was her everything but she went off and said i wont love anyone while you work on yourself but she went back to her last one i had to give up my time to heal just to get her back it hurt more then i ever thought i think thats why theres always was fighting not opening up and no love but i still tried but felt like maybe is it worth it will it get better will it change will i forget the damage done or will it not stop will the pain stay will i love the same again when you have 11 months to think you think of the stuff and you lose the love you once had you never turly heal from pain they made you feel and when that happens you think what could of done to change it could i of just not try to heal myself the healing i did in a week was not much but

the pain to come when i got you back was more then i thought
it would be i pushed threw it and tried to forget the wrongs
but the wrongs took over the rights the good time the times
we made we had a kid but that didnt fix much of us i tried to
be a better person for you but i never could my hearts heavy
my love is pure but the bandages keep opening and i cant
stop it i messed it up i blame all this on me would it be better
if i would of stayed would non of this happen if i didnt do
the things i did after it all we changed for the worst not for
the best /fear over rides alot of me with things like love and

without love i feel lost love like we had was strong made to be
but maybe it was not our time maybe it will be one day seeing
you smile cheering seeing you happy made me love more of
you but the good never took away the bad parts maybe i need
to heal before we love again or maybe it wont work love was
pure love is kind love is hard to find but we messed up along
the way or maybe it was all me maybe who knows we wont
ever find out cause when the past comes up the pain reopens
i still think of the late night things the christmas trip with
you we were cold me and your brother going at it on go karts
spinning him out it was racing maybe i watched to much
nascar and F1 but i wont forget it we had great times and bad
times but the good will be here but the bad is hard to fight
love is hard for us and always will be for us

XI

friends side of my life

I haven't known Jake for that long, however I have seen ups and down with his anxiety and depression. When I first met him I could see it. He really didn't even have to tell me. Over time as we kept talking I could see a positive change in his mood. But of course some days and nights hit lows. But he always pushed through and never gave up. He may have felt defeated at times but

I reminded him that God is by his side and that he is strong and I am here to listen when he needs someone to talk to and to pick him up when he falls. I would always pray for him when he was feeling down and I still do. I could see when he had good days and I was always happy to see that. Anxiety and depression will always have their ups and downs. But the sun will rise again in the morning so keep pushing and thank God for everything you have.

XII

the person that helps

i love my life now i have a great friend named raven shes been helping telling me it will be okay shes told me opening up is okay and helped me get my girl back and to keep pushing and shown me that not everyone is here in my life to hurt me and use me we talk alot shes great her heart is pure she never lets a day go by without jokes getting mad over games we play she always makes sure i am okay and that i push threw things helping me see that life is hard but with the right ones it is easy she cares alot about people shes the best person youll meet everyone needs some like her

she and i just got close but within those days we grew a bond i have not had in a while she supports me and pushes me to get this book done and that im a great dad she knows my struggles and fears but shes led me out of the darkness also showing me the world is not bad like i was thinking it was after everything happen in my life this year and that i need to keep my head up and not let things stop me shes been a huge help i hope she stays around and we stay close like we are

XIII

new start

now its late 2023 i have a a amazing son and now having another kid and i hope its a girl theres movies of dads with there girls and i want to be a girl dad i love my boy he is my everything and i want a girl in honer of my nana i hope its a girl i want 1 boy 1 girl with this girl i want to keep writing books and keep my head up and always love like i should i want to stay in my town but i want my boy and new kid to have a new start but if my health does not let me at least i know i can work here and keep doing books about my kids my love and my life this maybe the end of my book but it wont be my last.

Printed in the USA
CPSIA information can be obtained
at www.ICGtesting.com
CBHW071815060824
12792CB00056B/1102